Moreland, Arthur
    Dickens landmarks in London. Written
and illus. by the author, with a foreword
by Sir Henry Dickens, K.C. Haskell House,
1973.
        82 p. illus.
    Reprint of the 1931 ed.


1. Dickens, Charles, 1812-1870 - Homes
& haunts. 2.          Literary landmarks -
London. I.            Title.

# DICKENS LANDMARKS IN LONDON

# DICKENS LANDMARKS IN LONDON

WRITTEN AND ILLUSTRATED
BY
ARTHUR MORELAND

WITH A FOREWORD
BY
SIR HENRY F. DICKENS, K.C.

"When found, make a note of."

CAPTAIN CUTTLE.

HASKELL HOUSE PUBLISHERS LTD.
*Publishers of Scarce Scholarly Books*
NEW YORK. N. Y. 10012
1973

HASKELL HOUSE PUBLISHERS Ltd.

*Publishers of Scarce Scholarly Books*

280 LAFAYETTE STREET

NEW YORK. N. Y. 10012

Library of Congress Cataloging in Publication Data

Moreland, Arthur.
    Dickens landmarks in London.

    Reprint of the 1931 ed.
    1.  Dickens, Charles, 1812-1870--Homes and haunts.
2.  Literary landmarks--London.  I.  Title.
PR4584.M63 1973        823'.8                72-6291
ISBN 0-8383-1625-5

Printed in the United States of America

TO MY SISTERS
D. M. AND B. M.

# FOREWORD

MY father was essentially a Londoner. It is well known that at one time of his life, when he was restless at night and his mind was at work, he used to wander through the streets of London to tire himself out. It was also his habit at one time to make his way to the East End of London in company with a Police Inspector to visit the Thieves' Kitchens (which have long since disappeared) and the common lodging-houses existing at that time. It is not to be wondered at, therefore, that he should have given so large a space in his writings to the city that he loved so well. The present book, which has been most carefully prepared and which shows in the author a very thorough knowledge of Charles Dickens's works, purports to give an illustrated account of London as depicted by him in his various books. This task has been carried out in a pleasant and judicious manner, and so far as I can gather from a perusal of the manuscript can be relied upon for its accuracy.

We know that Sam Weller's knowledge of London was " extensive and peculiar." The same may, I think, be said of the author of this interesting work.

HENRY F. DICKENS.

# PREFACE

THE face of London is changing so rapidly that the time cannot be far distant when much that is recorded in these pages will have disappeared. So much has already gone that what remains is rendered thereby all the more precious, and every Dickens lover feels the destruction of still another relic, as he would the loss of an old friend.

The collection of evidence sufficient to identify what is left, is a fascinating puzzle to which Dickens's invariable use of actuality provides the key. The letter, quoted by Forster, in which he writes that he had been to Bevis Marks, " to look at a house for Sampson Brass," is a case in point.

How complete in every detail is this little household. Sampson himself either originated in one man Dickens had seen, or, as was sometimes the case, was a composite portrait of two or three ; but anyhow, he had lived, as had his entirely appropriate sister, Sally. This precious couple was provided with a foil drawn from Dickens's memory of his mother's little servant maid, the " Orfling," who now became the Marchioness.

To Dickens they were real and living people at the moment, without a home ; so he went to Bevis Marks, a street in which he would wish people whom he cordially disliked to live, and found the house. He must have gained admission, for it is described in particular detail. Instances of this same method occur in such regular sequence that it is safe to assume a fixed practice.

There is one within my own experience. That of Anthony Chuzzlewit's house in Foster Lane. Situated, as it is recorded, " in one of the narrow streets behind the Post Office," indicated without doubt either Foster Lane or Gutter Lane. The house, No. 5, Foster Lane, agrees in every detail with the description in Martin Chuzzlewit.

London is not big enough for the sum-total of Dickens lovers to live in, and, comparatively, only a few have that advantage. To them this book may act as an incentive to more voyages of discovery. Those to whom London is a vast and little known country will find the London of Dickens so arranged that, having found the starting-point, they should have no difficulty in following the route.

ARTHUR MORELAND.

LONDON. *July*, 1931.

# CONTENTS

# LIST OF ILLUSTRATIONS

# DICKENS LANDMARKS IN LONDON

## I

## Charing Cross, Adelphi and the Strand

CHARLES DICKENS lived and wrote in a great age of transition. The stage coach, the last relic of the good old leisurely times, was soon, with the advent of the railway, to yield before the era of speed. At the time of Dickens's birth we were, as regards social conditions, but little removed from the darkness of the Middle Ages.

The Law was brutally savage and mercilessly administered ; education, such as we know it, was thought not only unnecessary, but dangerous ; and the whole social system, rank and rotten from the highest to the lowest, offered a rich field to the reformer.

The son of John Dickens, a clerk in the Navy Pay Office, Charles John Huffam Dickens was born at Portsea on February 7, 1812. In 1814 his father was transferred to London, and from 1816 to 1821 he was at Chatham.

At the age of nine, Charles was brought back to London to live in Bayham Street, Camden Town, " a mean small tenement, with a wretched little back garden," marking the time when David Copperfield came to London to lodge with the Micawbers. The whole of *Copperfield* dealing with David's childhood in London to the time when, at the age of nineteen, he became a reporter of the Parliamentary debates, is the story of Dickens's own life.

Endowed to an extraordinary degree with the faculty of observation linked to a retentive memory, he found his material all around him. His life as a newspaper reporter trained him to record fact, and, in a sense, a reporter he remained from the first word he wrote to the last. There is strong proof that in delineating his characters he was drawing from living people, and the same applies to the places where they lived. For the simple reason that his surroundings provided all the material he needed, invention, as such, was automatically excluded, and from the time when he dropped his first contribution " through a letter-box up a dark court in Fleet Street," to the last words of *Edwin Drood*, it was fact, dressed in humour or tragedy, praise or withering scorn.

What Dickens wrote is for all to read and to judge how far he was directly responsible for leaving the world better than he found it.

The last thirty years have seen the destruction of much of London that Dickens knew, but there is sufficient surviving, to make it well worth while for the Dickens student to seek, and gratify his interest.

Let us begin at the hub of London, Charing Cross, and try to reconstruct it as it was on the morning of May 13, 1827, when Mr. Pickwick arrived at the Golden Cross Hotel to meet Mr. Tupman, Mr. Snodgrass and Mr. Winkle. Reference to the map

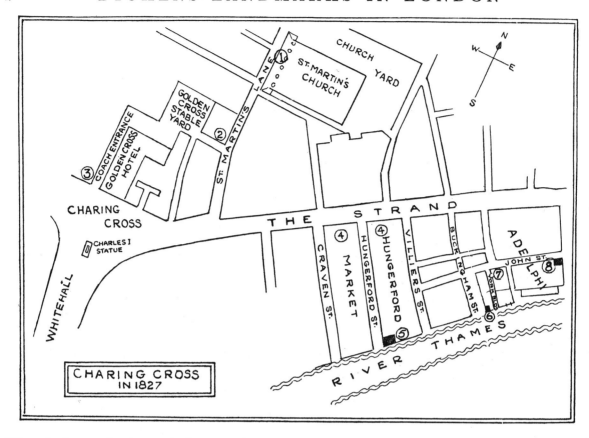

(No. 3) shows the hotel facing Whitehall, and about where is now the Nelson column. It was demolished two years later, when the space for Trafalgar Square was cleared. Its successor, built in the Strand, has recently suffered the same fate.  The space now occupied by the National Gallery and Trafalgar Square was covered with old houses, barracks, a mews, and the stable yard of the Golden Cross.  Charing Cross Road was not made and St. Martin's Lane, narrow and dark, ran down to the Strand.

Hereabouts the main interest is with David Copperfield.  David was at the time (Chap. XL) acting as secretary to his old schoolmaster, Dr. Strong, then living in retirement at Highgate, and was walking home to his rooms in Buckingham Street.  He says, " my shortest way home was through St. Martin's Lane.  Now, the Church which gives its name to the Lane, stood in a less free situation at that time, [*Copperfield* was written in 1849–50] there being no open space before it.  On the steps of the church, [Map, No. 1] there was the stooping figure of a man, who had put down some burden on the smooth snow, to adjust it.  I stood face to face with Mr. Peggotty."

Then comes one of the numerous instances of Dickens's exactness of detail.  " In those days there was a side entrance to the stable-yard of the Golden Cross nearly opposite to where we stood.  I pointed out the gateway [Map No. 2] and we went across."  They went into one of the public rooms opening off the inn yard, and David heard of Mr. Peggotty's fruitless journey in search of Little Em'ly, and his determination to set out again.

From here, we can trace David's way home.  Crossing the Strand, he would pass Craven Street on the right.  Down this street, at No. 39, is where a certain Dickens enthusiast declared that Mr. Brownlow, who befriended Oliver Twist, lived. There is no direct evidence to the truth of this, and it subsequently transpired that the then landlord (the house is now an hotel) was a friend of the would-be historian, and between them they made out quite a feasible case for No. 39 being Mr. Brownlow's dwelling. In its original state as a private house it is quite suitable, but there are several others with as good a claim on the same grounds, and all that we know is, that Mr. Brownlow lived in one of the houses in Craven Street.

From Craven Street you pass Charing Cross Station, where, in David's

St. Martin's Church
Trafalgar Square

Arthur Moreland 1931

time, stood Hungerford Market [Map, No. 4] intersected by Hungerford Street. At the foot of this street, near the river, was Jonathan Warren's Blacking Factory [Map, No. 5] where Dickens was put to work when ten years old. John Forster, Dickens's friend and biographer, records recollections of this time as related to him by Dickens. " In an evil hour for me, as I often bitterly thought, its chief manager, James Lambert, the relative who had lived with us in Bayham Street, seeing how I was employed from day to day, and knowing what our domestic circumstances then were, proposed that I should go into the blacking warehouse at a salary of six shillings a week. The offer was accepted very willingly by my father and mother, and on a Monday morning I went down to the blacking warehouse to begin my business life. It is wonderful to me how I could have been so easily cast away at such an age. It is wonderful to me that, even after my descent into the poor little drudge I had been since we came to London, no one had compassion enough on me—a child of singular abilities, quick, eager, delicate, and soon hurt, bodily or mentally—to suggest that something might have been spared, to place me at any common school. My father and mother were quite satisfied. They could hardly have been more so, if I had been twenty years of age, distinguished at a Grammar School, and going to Cambridge. The blacking warehouse was the last house on the left-hand side, at Old Hungerford stairs. [This would be about half-way beneath the present railway bridge.] It was a crazy, tumble-down old house, abutting on the river, and literally overrun with rats. The counting-house was on the first floor, looking over the coal barges and the river. [There was a coal wharf at the foot of Craven Street.] There was a recess in it, in which I was to sit and work. My work was to cover the pots of paste blacking ; first with a piece of oil paper, and then a piece of blue paper ; to tie them round with a string ; and then to clip the paper close and neat."

One of the other boys similarly employed was named Bob Fagin, " and," continues Dickens, " I took the liberty of using his name long afterwards in *Oliver Twist*." He tells how " words could not express the secret agony of my soul as I sank into this companionship. My whole nature was so penetrated with grief and humiliation, that even now, famous and caressed and happy, I often forget in my dreams that I have a dear wife and children ; even that I am a man ; and wander desolately back to that time of my life." [1]

This period is set forth in *David Copperfield* ; the blacking factory becoming Murdstone and Grinby's wine cellars, and the blacking bottles, wine bottles which David and the other boys washed. On the opposite side of the street from the blacking warehouse, was the " old public-house whose protruding wooden rooms overhung the river " where the Micawber family spent their last night in England before sailing for Australia (*Copperfield*, LVII).

Although all this has been swept away, it is worth while to go down there and, in imagination, take away the Embankment and railway bridge. You would see the shelving bank of the river, coming down until it met the mud ; above, the coal barges at the foot of Craven Street, the old houses of Hungerford Market and Villiers Street, while beyond, where are now the pleasant Embankment Gardens, the tide washed the foot of Adelphi Terrace, occasionally invading the Arches beneath.

From the Embankment you reach Villiers Street through the hall of Charing Cross Underground station. On your left is the viaduct of Charing Cross Southern Railway Station, the Eastern boundary of Hungerford Market. A few yards on the right, an iron gate, at the top of a flight of steps, leads to York Terrace, where, half-way down, is Buckingham Street. The stone gateway, now standing in the Embankment Gardens, at the foot of Buckingham Street, is the Water Gate of York House, the Duke of Buckingham's palace demolished in 1672. At the south-east corner [Map, No. 6], the angle of the Nurses' Pension Fund building occupies the site of No. 15, Buckingham Street, where, in 1834, Dickens had rooms on the top floor.

Here, undoubtedly, the landlady was the original Mrs. Crupp, David Copperfield's landlady (Chap. XXIII). David had just been articled to Spenlow and Jorkins of Doctors' Commons, and, with his aunt, Miss Trotwood, following the directions in the advertisement, applied to Mrs. Crupp at No. 15. She is introduced in a phrase

[1] Forster's *Life of Dickens*.

of thirteen words, a master-piece of description, " a stout lady with a flounce of flannel petticoat beneath a nankeen gown," a thumb-nail sketch that brings her to vivid reality. David's subsequent experiences with Mrs. Crupp are gems of comic writing. Her apparent association of David with washing day, by addressing him as " Mr. Copperfull "; her peculations indicated by the enormous quantities of tea and coffee that David apparently consumed, and the presence of something in the pantry that caused his brandy bottle to burst.

Buckingham Street

Except that this house has gone, Buckingham Street remains much the same as when Dickens lived there, to re-create it eleven years later when David took his place. His aunt, Betsey Trotwood, after her financial losses, lived with him there, Mr. Dick having a lodging in the nearby Hungerford Market. Mr. and Mrs. Micawber came there to dinner, this being the occasion when Mrs. Crupp produced a leg of mutton which had, apparently, been dropped into the ashes of the grate. Tommy Traddles was also a guest on this occasion. Peggotty and Mr. Peggotty, Uriah Heep, who, much to David's disgust, once slept there, and Steerforth came ; they have all walked down Buckingham Street, and it needs no great stretch of fancy to see them all again, on the way to, or from, the house that stands there no more.

Down the steps at the end of Buckingham Street, turning east to the end of York Terrace, another flight of steps leads to the cul-de-sac of York Buildings. A gate at the end on your right leads down to the old river-level of Adelphi Terrace and to one of the entrances to Adelphi Arches, " Lower Robert Street," surely one of the queerest " streets " in London, which leads to another entrance, at the Duke Street end of York Buildings [Map, No. 7]. In all probability, when Dickens, seeking respite from the blacking factory, used to wander through the arches, he would come this way, as the river-front would be practically inaccessible. The brothers Adam built the Adelphi, completing it in 1768, the arches, massively built of brick, forming the substructure.

Entrance to Adelphi Arches

Turning up Duke Street, which merges into John Street, leads to the Adelphi Hotel, "Osborne's Hotel," the London Headquarters of Mr. Wardle (*Pickwick*). Here, Mr. Pickwick announced his retirement, and the winding up of the Pickwick Club (Chap. LVII). Mr. Wardle's sitting-room, with the bedroom opening from it, would be the room lighted by the first two windows from the left on the first floor. This was the only apartment in the house with a connecting room; and the latter was the scene of the involuntary imprisonment of Mr. Snodgrass, when surprised by the unexpected return of Mr. Wardle (Chap. LIV). This room was demolished some years ago, to.

Adelphi Hotel
John Street

make way for a staircase ; otherwise, the house is unchanged, and has some fine Adam ceilings. A regrettable disfigurement of the exterior is the entirely incongruous glass porch, a gimcrack excrescence that should be removed.

Returning to the Strand by way of Adam Street and turning east, Strand Lane will be found on the right, through a covered way, opposite the Church of St. Mary le Strand. Here is a relic of Roman London, the famous Roman bath. Dickens often bathed in it, and David Copperfield says that he went there and plunged into the coldest water in London. Originally, it was the bath of a Roman house, and has been there for over sixteen hundred years. The Roman bricks round the edge of the bath might have been set yesterday, so firm and perfect are they. A tank for fresh water supply is still in place at the foot, being fed by a spring. Nowadays, the water runs away through waste pipes, into the sewers.

A few yards further east, on the same side of the Strand, is Essex Street, formerly part of the Outer Temple, a portion of the ancient wall of which is intersected by the steps at the end of the street, leading down to the river-level. The gateway closing the end of the street is the watergate of Essex House, another of the palaces that, in Elizabeth's time, fringed the Strand as far as Westminster.

Most of the old houses in Essex Street have been demolished, the most notable exception being the Watergate.  In one of the houses on the left, the actual one has probably been pulled down, Magwitch, the escaped convict in *Great Expectations* found a hiding-place.  In Chapter XL, Pip says, " There being to my knowledge a respectable lodging-house in Essex Street, the back of which looked into the Temple, and was almost within hail of my windows."  Here, Magwitch under the name of Provis lay concealed.

Of the Strand, along which we have just passed, hardly a building that Dickens saw remains.  The change is still in rapid progress ; day by day the face of London alters, and will continue to do so, until all its familiar features will have vanished.

Essex Street. Strand.

Arthur Moreland 1921

9

# II

# The Temple and Fleet Street

THE substitution of the new for the old in a city around which the world's money revolves is inevitable. With few exceptions Dickens, if he could be placed at any point within a mile of Charing Cross, would be compelled to apply to the point policeman for guidance.

In the course of this chronicle it will be necessary, at almost every point, to refer to some change or other where London has lost a dignified, and often beautiful old age, to assume the modern attire of concrete, fitted with brazenly staring windows; while within, instead of toiling up wooden staircases protected by a broad balustrade of oak (until the King's ships put in a prior claim and compelled the substitution of deal), we enter a cage, where the man in charge presses a button, and we are in, and out, our business completed, while our grandfather would probably be on the second landing, regaining his breath and rubbing his shin, having slipped and stumbled on the worn and ill-lighted stairway.

The Strand, down which we are passing, contains few if any buildings that were there when Dickens last walked along it. He would look in vain for his old news-paper office, and for the house where Miss La Creevy, the miniature painter in *Nicholas Nickleby*, lived. Imagine anybody living in the Strand nowadays; but she found it convenient, for, as she observed, there were so many people passing that if she wanted a particular type of nose for a miniature, she would be sure to see it on looking out of the window. A glance down Norfolk Street instantly reveals the impossibility of Mrs. Lirriper's lodgings being there to-day.

Our last point was Essex Street, and still going eastward along the Strand, we pass the Law Courts which stand on part of the site of Clare Market, swept away, together with the dreadful slums in the Drury Lane area, years ago. Almost opposite the end of Chancery Lane stands the Temple Gate House, built by Christopher Wren in 1684. Dickens mentions it frequently and many of his characters have passed through the Gate.

In *Martin Chuzzlewit* (XXXIX) John Westlock called on Tom Pinch at his lodg-ings in Islington, and told a story of a visit he had had from a mysterious gentleman who appeared to know that Mr. Pinch stood in need of employment, and that he was commissioned by a client, whose name he was not at liberty to divulge, to offer Tom a situation as a "sort of secretary." The gentleman's card, which John Westlock produced, bore the name of "Mr. Fips, Austin Friars, and there he expects us to call this morning," said John.

To Austin Friars they went—it is now rebuilt—found Mr. Fips, who, except for the information that he could instal Tom in his new employment, was mysteriously uncommunicative. "The place is in the Temple," said Mr. Fips, and on Tom expressing a wish to see the place, Mr. Fips made an appointment to meet Tom and Mr. Westlock at the Temple Gate in Fleet Street.

They would go down Middle Temple Lane which contains some of the oldest houses in the Temple, their overhanging stories towering above the narrow Lane. These few houses near the gate are all that is left of the old Middle Temple Lane, and the modern buildings occupying the rest of its length date from the nineteenth century, that period of universal vandalism, which produced a species of ponderous Gothic of which you see a sample where the old houses end ; as incongruous a mixture as could be contrived. Elm Court, on the left, provides yet another instance of depressing ugliness. There is a remaining fragment of one of the old buildings, enough to indicate the simple dignity of the original, and to show how really hideous these Victorian buildings could be. Elm Court looks its best on a wet day with an east wind cutting through the narrow passage leading to Inner Temple.

Mr. Fips and his two companions were not bound for Elm Court but for Pump Court, which, with the exception of a small excrescence in the north-east corner, probably the work of the artist of Elm Court—it might have been Mr. Pecksniff himself—remains much the same to-day as it was when Mr. Fips conducted John Westlock and Tom Pinch to the upper story of one of these old houses. Mr. Fips stopped at a door which had a smear of paint where custom would have placed the tenant's name. The room was

North Gate Middle Temple

Middle Temple Lane

Arthur Moreland.
1931

filled with lumber, mouldering furniture, and piles of books everywhere, the whole covered with the dust of years. Mr. Fips suggested that the first thing to be done was to have these latter arranged and catalogued and then, having arranged

Pump Court
Middle Temple

Arthur
Moreland.
1931

for Tom to call at Austin Friars every week for his salary, he abruptly took his departure.

Tom entered upon his entirely congenial employment, and spent many happy studious days, pausing now and again to wonder and speculate upon the identity of his employer. In Chapter L Tom is at work when a step on the stairs attracts his attention.

" ' Ah ! ' said Tom, looking towards the door, ' time was, and not long ago either, when that would have set me wondering and expecting. But I have left off now.'

" The footstep came on, up the stairs.

" ' Thirty-six, thirty-seven, thirty-eight,' said Tom, counting. ' Now you'll stop. Nobody ever comes past the thirty-eighth stair.' "

A moment afterwards old Martin Chuzzlewit stood in the doorway, and perhaps what is the most powerful book that Dickens wrote is nearing its climax. In Chapter LII the story continues. Old Martin had taken up his quarters in Pump Court and was attended by Mr. Mark Tapley, who was to open the door to visitors, being expressly requested not to show surprise at their appearance. There was to be a considerable strain upon Mr. Tapley's powers of self-control, for a remarkable company were about to pass through the Temple Gate and down the Lane. First came John Westlock, closely followed by Tom Pinch and his sister. Then young Martin, the old man scarcely looking at him, pointing to a distant seat. Another knock heralded the arrival of Mary Graham and Mrs. Lupin. The strangeness of this assemblage was marked by the evident surprise that everybody showed at the sight of everybody else. The silence was broken by old Martin.

" ' Set the door open, Mark ! ' he said, ' and come here.'

" The last appointed footstep sounded now upon the stairs. They all knew it. It was Mr. Pecksniff's ; and Mr. Pecksniff was in a hurry too, for he came bounding up with such uncommon expedition that he stumbled twice or thrice.

" ' Where is my venerable friend ? ' he cried, upon the upper landing ; and then with open arms came darting in."

We all know what followed. Pecksniff felled to the floor by a vigorous blow from old Martin's stick which, as Mr. Pecksniff observed in his subsequent valedictory address, he " had every reason to believe had knobs upon it."

Though no direct reference is made to Pump Court, it is generally supposed to be the place chosen by Dickens as the scene of the final extinction of Pecksniff.

It is important to keep in mind the invariable practice of Dickens, after drawing his characters from life, to place them in surroundings with which he was familiar. In a letter to John Forster, written in 1840 when he was writing *The Old Curiosity Shop*, Dickens says, " I intended calling on you this morning on my way back from Bevis Marks, whither I went to look at a house for Sampson Brass." In Chapter XXXIII of *The Old Curiosity Shop* the house, outside and inside, is described with his accustomed wealth of detail. The same thing occurs again and again, and points conclusively to

Fountain Court Middle Temple

the fact that his characters were so real to him, living men and women, that they had to live in real houses.

A few yards down Middle Temple Lane brings us to Fountain Court. Middle Temple Hall, dating from 1562, occupies the south side of the Court. Dickens entered his name as a student at the Middle Temple in 1838, though he did not eat dinners there until many years later.

The Court is associated with John Westlock's courtship of Ruth Pinch, and is much the same to-day as when Ruth Pinch waited by the fountain for her brother, so that she might walk home with him.  John Westlock often seemed to have business there, at about the same time ; and in *Chuzzlewit* (LIII) John meets Ruth to some purpose, and " Fiery Face," John's laundress at his chambers in Furnival's Inn, loses her situation.

5 King's Bench Walk.
Inner Temple

FLEET ST.

Inner Temple Gate

Arthur
Moreland.
1931

It was quite natural that they should glance down Garden Court ; because Garden Court ends in the Garden, and the Garden ends in the River, and that glimpse is very bright and fresh and shining on a summer's day. It still is ; the only changes being that the gardens are now separated from the River by the Embankment ; the old buildings that once nearly reached the river, and where Pip in *Great Expectations* had his chambers, have been substituted by stone buildings of a florid style of architecture difficult to classify ; but distance softens the discordant note they strike against the old buildings that remain at the northern end.

From Fountain Court we recross Middle Temple Lane, and passing through Elm Court enter Inner Temple, the eastern boundary of which is formed by King's Bench Walk.

Mr. Stryver, the hard-drinking, bullying barrister in *A Tale of Two Cities*, is supposed to have lived at No. 3, though there is no direct evidence to establish identification. The doorways of these houses, probably designed by Christopher Wren, are famous specimens of carved brickwork, the bricks being carved after they were set. During one of his periods of prosperity, Oliver Goldsmith lived at No. 3.

The Inner Temple Gate is the scene of Bradley Headstone's watch over the movements of Eugene Wrayburn. In *Our Mutual Friend* (XXVI–XXVII) Eugene Wrayburn tells Mortimer Lightwood how Bradley Headstone, consumed with jealousy and hate, lurks in dark doorways watching for Eugene to come out by the Gate, then to follow him to be sure, whether or not, he is seeking Lizzie Hexam. Eugene takes long nocturnal walks, leading the unhappy schoolmaster by devious ways all over London. "Night after night," says Eugene, "his disappointment is acute, but hope springs eternal in the scholastic breast, and he follows me again to-morrow. When I do not enjoy the pleasures of the chase, for all I know he watches the Temple Gate all night."

The Inner Temple East Gate figures in at least two specific references. In *Our Mutual Friend* (XII) Rogue Riderhood is in Mortimer Lightwood's chambers in the Temple, hinting that he has evidence as to the murder of John Harmon. Mortimer and Eugene decide to test Riderhood's information by going to Limehouse.

" ' Let us walk,' whispered Lightwood, ' and give this fellow time to think of it.'

" The waterside character pulled his drowned cap over his ears with both hands, and making himself more round-shouldered than nature had made him, went down the stairs, round by the Temple Church, across the Temple into Whitefriars, and so on by the waterside streets."

It is only possible to follow their route as far as Blackfriars, for where they would slope down to the river-level the Underground Railway Station stands, and Queen Victoria Street cuts across to join the Embankment. The only remaining trace of the old narrow streets then running down to the river is Water Lane, behind Ludgate Hill Station. Queen Victoria Street now marks its end, and the Underground Railway runs over its old termination at the river-level.

Passing in the reverse direction over the same route Pip, in *Great Expectations* (XLIV), on his way from London Bridge walks to his chambers in Garden Court. He says, " My readiest access to the Temple was close by the river-side through Whitefriars." The night porter at the gate had a letter for him, which bore on the outside the words

The Inner Temple East Gate

Arthur Moreland.
1931.

" Please read this here." Pip opened it and, by the light of the porter's lantern, read, in Wemmick's writing : " Don't go home."

After passing through the Gate, on the left is Bouverie Street, where Dickens founded the *Daily News* in December 1845. In a note written at six o'clock in the morning of January 21, 1846, he tells John Forster that they had " been at press three-quarters of an hour, and were out before *The Times*." Another note written in the night

Hanging Sword
Alley

of 9th of February, "tired to death and quite worn out," he tells Forster that he had resigned the Editorship. His renewed connexion with journalism lasted less than three weeks, and, although he made occasional contributions to the paper, Fleet Street was not to his liking. One wonders what his opinion of it would be nowadays.

Turning up Whitefriars Street leading to Fleet Street, a flight of steps on the right leads to Hanging Sword Alley, where that "honest tradesman" Mr. Jerry Cruncher in *A Tale of Two Cities*, had his private lodging. All traces of Mr. Cruncher's other dwellings in the Alley have long since disappeared, and it now serves as a narrow breathing-space between towering newspaper offices. It was known at one time as Blood Bowl Alley from the notorious Blood Bowl House.

Crossing Fleet Street, Wine Office Court leads to the Cheshire Cheese. In *A Tale of Two Cities* (IV), Sydney Carton takes Charles Darnay, after the trial at the Old Bailey, " down Ludgate-hill to Fleet-street, and so, up a covered way into a tavern." Without a doubt the Cheshire Cheese, very little altered to-day to what it was when Darnay " recruited his strength with a good plain dinner and good wine."

The house is well cared for, even to such a detail as the refusal of the proprietor to renew the doorstep, which Carton and Darnay's feet probably helped to wear, covering it for safety's sake with an iron grating. Dickens, for some reason known to himself, does not mention the house by name, though he knew it well enough and dined there more than once.

Further west on the same side of Fleet Street is the gateway of Clifford's Inn. In *Our Mutual Friend* (VIII), John Rokesmith follows Mr. Boffin down Fleet Street, speaks to him and suggests that they, for quietness, turn into Clifford's Inn, and there Rokesmith proposes himself as Mr. Boffin's secretary.

Dickens describes the Inn as a " mouldy little plantation or cat preserve " and does not appear to be at all impressed by its undeniable picturesqueness. He is, in fact, strangely insensible to the beauty of Old London ; there was much more of it in his day, but he was so concerned with the state of the slums and the misery of the people who crowded them, that these old places held no appeal to his senses. Much of Clifford's Inn has gone, and what remains was purchased some years ago by a firm of printers, and the day will not long be deferred before it will be swept away. A particularly fine block of buildings abutting on the grounds of the Rolls Office has been purchased by the Government as a " fire screen," and is doomed to destruction when it becomes necessary to build an additional wing to the Rolls Office. These houses date from the sixteenth century and contain several of the original Tudor windows.

The Cheshire Cheese
Wine Office Court

Clifford's Inn, together with Thavies, Furnival's, Staple, Barnard's and Clement's
Inns, were known as Inns of Chancery. They were distinct from, and subsidiary to, the

four Inns of Court, namely Middle Temple, Inner Temple, Lincoln's Inn and Gray's Inn, and were used as preparatory schools ; boys being sent thither to receive an education which was intended to train them to become members of an Inn of Court, which, in turn, trained them to become barristers.

Serjeants' Inn was not an Inn of Chancery. The degree of Serjeant-at-law (now obsolete) was superior to that of barrister-at-law. Serjeants were the only advocates entitled to audience in the Court of Common Pleas, and they sat within the bar of the Court like a K.C. It was the practice to appoint none but Serjeants to the Bench, hence an outer barrister, who was about to be made a judge, was always first made a Serjeant, when he became automatically a member of Serjeants' Inn.

The Serjeants abandoned their first hall in Chancery Lane—a tablet on the wall a few yards up from Fleet Street marks the site—and built New Serjeants' Inn in Fleet Street. The old hall was then used as Judges' Chambers and Mr. Pickwick appeared here on the writ obtained by Dodson & Fogg. On being satisfied that he had been duly taken in execution, the judge made an order that he be committed to the Fleet Prison.

Clifford's Inn
Fleet Street

Arthur
Moreland.
1931

23

58 Lincoln's Inn Fields

Arthur
Moreland.
1931

# III

## Lincoln's Inn, Chancery Lane and Holborn

A LITTLE way down Kingsway a turning on the right by the London Opera House, now a cinema, leads you to Lincoln's Inn Fields. An old house in Portsmouth Street bears on its front an announcement in large letters that it is " the original Old Curiosity Shop, immortalized by Charles Dickens." This is not correct, for when Dickens knew Portsmouth Street there were many old houses standing of which this was one ; and the probability is that at that time it was not a shop, but a dwelling-house. The original of the Old Curiosity Shop was either in Green Street, Leicester Square, or in Fetter Lane, but, in either case, both places were demolished many years ago.

At No. 58 Lincoln's Inn Fields lived Dickens's friend and biographer, John Forster. " It had been," says Dickens, " a house of State, but had fallen somewhat from its former grandeur, and was let off in suites of rooms." It was here that Sir Leicester Dedlock's lawyer, Mr. Tulkinghorn, lived, and here he was found shot dead, with the Roman on the painted ceiling pointing towards him as he lay, face downwards, on the floor (*Bleak House*, XLVII). There is now no trace of a painted ceiling in the house, nor any evidence of there having ever been one. It is still a fine old house and was built at the end of the seventeenth century when Lincoln's Inn Fields was a fashionable residential quarter.

It is best to walk across the Fields through Lincoln's Inn to Chancery Lane, where the famous gate-house, smoke-blackened and grim, forms the chief entrance to the Inn. It leads to Old Square, which including the sites of the Old Hall and Chapel formed the town residence of the Bishops of Chichester. In 1227 one of the Bishops, Ralph de Neville, was also Lord Chancellor, and after he had built himself a house, the street leading to it was called Chancellor's Lane, from which it appears that Chancery Lane did not have an entirely legal origin. The original gate-house of the Bishops' Palace stood further south than the present one, which was completed in 1522. It was erected at a total cost of £345, of which Sir Thomas Lovell, K.G., contributed one-third. His coat of arms appears on the tablet over the central arch of the gate.

At No. 8 New Square, in 1826 and 1827, Dickens was a clerk in the offices of Mr. Molloy, a solicitor.

In *Bleak House* (III) Esther Summerson says " we drove through the dirtiest and darkest streets that ever were seen in the world, and in such a distracting state of confusion that I wondered how the people kept their senses, until we passed into sudden quietude under an old gateway, and drove on through a silent square until we came to an odd nook in a corner, where there was an entrance up a steep, broad flight of stairs, like an entrance to a church.

This was where Mr. Kenge, of Kenge and Carboy, had his office. This part of Old Square was rebuilt in 1880, that fatal period already referred to when the peculiar form of Gothic shown in the small illustration was substituted for the sixteenth-century buildings, similar to those still standing in the southern part of Old Square. Some recent restorations there, of the house, and staircase tower at the southern end of the Old Hall, show the desire of the present authorities of the Inn to preserve the original design, for the house was carefully rebuilt exactly as it had formerly stood, and as much as possible of the old material was used.

13 Old Square
Lincoln's Inn     Arthur Moreland

We now come to the Old Hall, built 1489–92, and now, after a period of dreadful disfigurement lasting from 1819 to 1928, restored both without and within to its original state.

The nineteenth century saw the introduction of stucco and the architects of the period seem to have treated brickwork like silver in the days of Solomon, as of no account. If they could not use stone they covered the offending brickwork with stucco. Having, by this method, "improved" the outward appearance of the Hall, they turned their attention to the interior.

It was "elegantly and commodiously improved" by being lengthened ten feet, and by the addition of a coved plaster ceiling, in order to conceal the

The Old Hall Lincoln's Inn
as it was from 1818 to 1928

The Gatehouse. Lincoln's Inn.
Chancery Lane

Arthur
Moreland
1931

27

offending Tudor roof timbers.   It remained in this state until 1925, when the Benchers of the Inn resolved to restore it.   After three years' work, under the direction of Sir John Simpson, K.B.E., the Old Hall threw off its disguise and appeared in its original form. This was a notable piece of restoration, in addition to being evidence that in our day these ancient monuments will be carefully and reverently preserved.[1]

From 1734 to the opening of the present Law Courts in the Strand, the Old Hall was the Lord Chancellor's Court and was the scene of the chancery case of Jarndyce and Jarndyce in *Bleak House* round which the novel is written.

Until about thirty years ago there were several definite places connected with *Bleak House*.   Star Yard, a narrow passage, runs from Carey Street along the length of the eastern boundary wall of the Inn.   Chichester Rents (another relic of the Bishops of Chichester), also a narrow passage, connects Star Yard with Chancery Lane.   All the old houses in Star Yard and Chichester Rents have been pulled down and modern buildings erected.

Krook, who blew up in spontaneous combustion, had his marine store in Star Yard, while poor Miss Flite lodged in a room over it, from the window of which she derived satisfaction from the view of the roof of the Old Hall which it afforded her. At the corner of Chichester Rents and Star Yard was the Old Ship Tavern, the Sol's Arms of the novel, where the Harmonic Meetings were held, the harmony being contributed by a gentleman named Swills and a lady " Miss M. Melvilleson, the noted syren," who was supposed by Mrs. Perkins and Mrs. Piper, two ladies residing in the immediate neighbourhood, to be married and to have her baby " clandestinely conveyed to the Sol's Arms every night to receive its natural nourishment during the entertainments " (*Bleak House*, XXXII).

Cursitor Street, on the opposite side of Chancery Lane from the gate-house, has been almost entirely re-built.   The first turn on the left is Took's Court, " Cook's Court " of *Bleak House*.   Here Mr. Snagsby lived and carried on his business as a Law Stationer.   His house must have been at or near the corner of the Court and Cursitor Street, for, from his shop-window, he could look down that thoroughfare.   Here also lived Mrs. Snagsby, as severe as Mr. Snagsby was mild.   A frequent guest was Mrs. Snagsby's favourite divine, evidently of some denomination of which he was the sole proprietor. In Chapter XIX, Dickens introduces him with one of his inimitable thumb-nail portraits: " Mr. Chadband is a large yellow man with a fat smile, and a general appearance of having a good deal of train oil in his composition."   Guster, the servant girl, subject to fits, is another character ;   the household and its visitors provide one of those patches of comedy where the genius of Dickens shines at its brightest.

Took's Court is interesting, inasmuch that the few houses down one side are the last remaining fragments of what was, a hundred years ago, a large residential district. When one of the houses was recently pulled down there one of its carved brick pilasters

---

[1] The drawing of the Old Hall, before restoration, is made from a photograph reproduced in a brochure published by the Benchers of the Inn at the time of the re-opening of the Old Hall by H.M. the Queen in 1928.   My grateful acknowledgments are due to the Benchers for their kindness in allowing me to reproduce it, together with many of the particulars recorded above.

The Old Hall
Lincoln's Inn.
Restored 1928

Arthur
Moreland
1931

29

was acquired by South Kensington Museum. Similar houses stood in Cursitor Street, but they have gone long ago, and it will not be many years before those left in Took's Court follow them.

Furnival Street at the end of Cursitor Street leads to Holborn. There, on the opposite side of the way, an immense red-brick building covers the site of Furnival's Inn, where Dickens lived in 1836 and where the first chapters of *Pickwick* were written. A few yards to the left the black and white front of Staple Inn faces the end of Gray's Inn Road. In *Edwin Drood* (XI) is this description: "Behind the most ancient part of Holborn, where certain gabled houses some centuries of age still stand looking on the public way, is a little nook composed of two irregular quadrangles, called Staple Inn. It is one of those nooks, the turning into which out of the clashing street, imparts to the relieved pedestrian the sensation of having put cotton in his ears, and velvet soles on his boots.

No. 10 Staple Inn

It is one of those nooks where a few smoky sparrows twitter in smoky trees, as though they called to one another, ' let us play at country.' . . . A set of chambers in a corner house in the little inner quadrangle, presenting in black and white over its ugly portal the mysterious inscription :

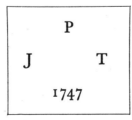

in which set of chambers, never having troubled his head about the inscription, unless to bethink himself at odd times on glancing up at it, that haply it might mean Perhaps John Thomas, or Perhaps Joe Tyler, sat Mr. Grewgious writing by his fire."

This is one of the few places, other than a public building, that Dickens specifically mentions. His description of the Inn, and the curious effect of the sudden silence, holds good to-day : the old place is remarkably well preserved, the original cobble-stones pavement adding not a little to its picturesqueness. The description of the door-way of No. 10 as an " ugly portal " is another instance of his lack of appreciation for what is a typical example of late seventeenth or early eighteenth-century architecture, well proportioned, simple and dignified. Dozens of ugly portals, built two centuries after this one, abound in the modern buildings near by in Holborn.

Another Inn of Chancery now claims attention. Thavies Inn, opening from St. Andrew's Street by Holborn Circus. Street improvements have left but this small portion, which contains a few of the original houses. Mr. Jellyby, who suffered, together with the rest of the household, from Mrs. Jellyby's preoccupation on behalf of the natives of Borrioboola-Gha, lived, probably, at No. 8. The description of the introduction of the Jellybys in *Bleak House* (IV) is one of Dickens's gems of comic writing. Esther Summerson was at Kenge & Carboy's office at 13, Old Square, Lincoln's Inn, together with Richard Carstone and Miss Clare, and they were to lodge that night at the Jellybys'. Mr. Kenge's clerk, " the young man of the name of Guppy," was directed to see them safely there.

" ' Where *is* " there," Mr. Guppy ? ' said Richard, as we went downstairs.

" ' No distance,' said Mr. Guppy ; ' round in Thavies Inn, you know. Only round the corner ; we just twist up Chancery-Lane, and cut along Holborn, and there we are in four minutes' time, as near as a toucher. This is about a London particular now, ain't it, Miss ? ' [Mr. Guppy was referring to the fog.] He seemed quite delighted with it on my account. . . .

" We turned up under an archway [this has gone] to our destination : a narrow street of high houses, like an oblong cistern to hold the fog. There was a confused little crowd of people, principally children, gathered about the house at which we stopped, which had a tarnished brass plate on the door, with the inscription, JELLYBY.

" ' Don't be frightened ' ! said Mr. Guppy, looking in at the coach-window. ' One of the young Jellybys has been and got his head through the area railings ! ' "

Young Jellyby having been released, the party entered the house, being admitted by a " person in pattens " ; who led them upstairs, past several more children whom it was difficult to avoid treading on in the dark, and as they were announced to Mrs. Jellyby as " them two young ladies," one of the children was heard to fall downstairs, judging by the noise, down a whole flight. Mrs. Jellyby did not appear to be at all disturbed, she received them with a far-away look, as far, probably, as Africa—and they sat down on " a lame invalid of a sofa." " Mrs. Jellyby had very good hair but was too much occupied with her African duties to brush it. The shawl in which she had been loosely muffled, dropped on to her chair when she advanced to meet us ; and as she turned to resume her seat, we could not help noticing that her dress didn't nearly meet up the back, and that the open space was railed across with a lattice work of stay-lace—like a summer house."

Mr. Kenge had previously stated, in answer to an inquiry, that he was not acquainted with Mr. Jellyby, had never seen him. "He may be," said Mr. Kenge, "a very superior man ; but he is, so to speak, merged—Merged—in the more shining qualities of his wife." This was indeed the case, and poor Mr. Jellyby's state of mind is indicated by the fact that near where he was accustomed to sit, there was a black patch on the wall, on the spot where he found it necessary to rest his head.

Ely Place is another of London's once fashionable quarters that have fallen to the level of offices and business premises of various de-

No 8 Thavie's Inn

Arthur Moreland 1931

scriptions. In *David Copperfield* (XXV), David received a note from Agnes, saying that she is staying at the house of her father's agent, Mr. Waterbrook, in Ely Place, Holborn. She asks David to call and see her ; he does so and meets Mrs. Waterbrook, who invites him to dinner next day. There are several of the thumbnail portraits in the account of the dinner-party. Mr. Waterbrook, "a middle-aged gentleman, with a short throat, and a good deal of shirt-collar, who only wanted a black nose to be the portrait of a pug dog." David was presented to "a very awful lady in a black velvet dress, and a great black velvet hat, whom I remember as looking like a near relation of Hamlet's—say his aunt." This was Mrs. Henry Spiker, Mr. Spiker being a solicitor remotely connected with the Treasury and, in consequence, was treated with immense deference. David also renewed his acquaintance with his old school-fellow, Tommy Traddles.

Mr. Waterbrook was extremely condescending to Traddles ; and David learned that it was only by the accident of Mrs. Henry Spiker's brother being suddenly indisposed, that Traddles was there at all, and had only been invited

Ely Place

that morning. Mr. Waterbrook suddenly switched off Traddles by observing, "A very gentlemanly man, Mrs. Henry Spiker's brother, Mr. Copperfield." Uriah Heep was also there, and there is the first hint of his gradual ascendancy over Mr. Wickfield.

# IV

## Gray's Inn, City Road and Somers Town

THE Holborn entrance to Gray's Inn was, in David Copperfield's time, part of Gray's Inn Coffee House, actually an hotel that had retained this description dating from the previous century.

David Copperfield describes in Chapter LIX his arrival in London from abroad and his drive to Gray's Inn Coffee House, on a wintry autumn evening. In the coffee-room, he inquires of the waiter where Mr. Traddles lived in the Inn. "Holborn Court, sir. Number two," said the waiter, and on David asking him whether Mr. Traddles's reputation among the lawyers was not rising, the waiter looked for help to a waiter of more authority, " a stout, potential old man, with a double-chin, in black breeches and stockings who came out of a place like a churchwarden's pew, at the end of the coffee-room, where he kept company with a cash-box, a Directory, a Law-list, and other books and papers."

The portentous waiter had never heard Mr. Traddles's name, and on learning that Traddles had been in the Inn for but a paltry three years, refused to pursue such an insignificant subject, and asked David what he would have for **dinner**.

On going to his bedroom to change his clothes, he remarks upon " the vast extent of the old wainscotted room, which was over the archway leading to the Inn." This part of the Holborn front has not met with any external alteration ; the square bay windows are exactly the same, overhanging the archway, as they have been for the last 300 years or so. The Coffee House has departed long ago, together with its massive four-post bedsteads, and the rooms are now offices of one description and another.

When David had finished his dinner, he determined to call on Traddles, and went out by the back way—the disused door may still be seen on the right-hand side under the arch—and the narrow lane would lead him to Holborn Court, or South Square, as it is now named.

" Number two in the Court was soon reached, and an inscription on the door-post informing me that Mr. Traddles occupied a set of chambers on the top story, I ascended the staircase. A crazy old staircase I found it to be, feebly lighted on each landing by a club-headed little oil wick, dying away in a little dungeon of dirty glass."

As he got nearer, David heard sounds of laughter, " not the laughter of an attorney or barrister but of two or three merry girls," and at this point he stumbled by putting his foot in a hole where " the Honourable Society of Gray's Inn had left a plank deficient," and the laughter at once subsided.

" Groping my way more carefully, I found the outer door, which had MR. TRADDLES

Holborn Gate, Gray's Inn.

painted on it, open. I knocked. A considerable scuffling within ensued, but nothing else. I therefore knocked again. A small sharp-looking lad, who was very much out of breath, but who looked at me as if he defied me to prove it legally, presented himself.

" ' Is Mr. Traddles within ? ' I said.

" ' Yes, sir, but he's engaged.'

" ' I want to see him ! '

" After a moment's survey of me, the sharp-looking lad decided to let me in; and opening the door wider for that purpose, admitted me, first, into a little closet of a hall, and next into a little sitting-room; where I came into the presence of my old friend (also out of breath), seated at a table, and bending over papers."

David was rapturously received by Traddles and learned that, at last, he and the dearest girl in the world were married, and the laughter David had heard proceeded from his wife and five of her sisters who were staying with them. David wondered how so many could be accommodated in so small a space of three rooms, but Traddles explained that " Sophy was a wonderful manager," as indeed she must have been.

The description of the rooms is exact, and they remain practically the same to-day, except that nowadays the Honourable Society of Gray's Inn look well after their property and there are now no ill-lighted staircases or missing boards.

It is highly probable that Dickens's friend, Judge Talfourd, was largely the original of Traddles, and that, as a young barrister, he lived in these chambers. Mr. Phunky, the junior to Serjeant Snubbin, Mr. Pickwick's leading Counsel in Bardell v. Pickwick, also had chambers here, and it was along the pavement in front of these buildings that he, with Mr. Perker and Mr. Pickwick, walked up and down in consultation.

Leaving South Square by the short passage on the left, we come to Field Court, which faces Gray's Inn Gardens. At the end of Field Court a turn to the right along the west side of the Gardens leads to Raymond Buildings, where, at No. 1, at the age of fifteen, Dickens was clerk to Ellis & Blackmore, on the second floor. In Chapter III of Forster's *Life*, some interesting particulars are given by Mr. Edward Blackmore, who writes : " I was well acquainted with his parents, and, being then in practice in Gray's Inn, they asked me if I could find employment for him. He was a bright, clever-looking youth, and I took him as a clerk. He came to me in May, 1827, and left in November, 1828 ; and I have now an account book which he used to keep of petty disbursements in the office, in which he charged himself with the modest salary of thirteen shillings and sixpence, and afterwards of fifteen shillings a week. Several incidents took place in the office, of which he must have been a keen observer, as I recognized

South Square
Gray's Inn.

Arthur
Moreland. 1931

some of them in his *Pickwick* and *Nickleby* ; and I am much mistaken if some of his characters have not their originals in persons I well remember."

Considering the settled practice of Dickens to " draw from life," do not these remarks of Mr. Blackmore's suggest that either he, or his partner Mr. Ellis, bore some resemblance to Mr. Perker, Mr. Pickwick's attorney ? Mr. Perker's office is said to have been at some number not stated, in Gray's Inn Square, but it seems that there is more reason for supposing that No. 1 Raymond Buildings was Mr. Perker's Gray's Inn address. If this is so, the office was the scene of Mr. Pickwick's last meeting with Messrs. Dodson and Fogg in Chapter LIII.

" ' You are a couple of mean, rascally, pettifogging robbers ! ' said Mr. Pickwick. ' Robbers ! ' cried Mr. Pickwick, running to the stair-head, as the two attorneys descended. ' Robbers ! ' shouted Mr. Pickwick, breaking from Lowten and Perker, and thrusting his head out of the staircase window. When Mr. Pickwick drew in his head again, his countenance was smiling and placid ; and, walking quietly back into the office, he declared that he had now removed a great weight from his mind, and

No. 48 Doughty Street

No. 1 Raymond Buildings
Gray's Inn.

Arthur
Moreland.
1931

that he felt perfectly comfortable and happy." The staircase window referred to is the second over the doorway.

Leaving the Inn by the near-by gate, John Street is almost opposite and the continuation of John Street is Doughty Street, where, at No. 48, Dickens lived from

March, 1837, to December, 1839. *Pickwick* was completed here, *Oliver Twist* and *Nicholas Nickleby* written and *Barnaby Rudge* commenced.

This period of a little under three years, before he had completed his thirtieth year, firmly established him as a literary genius. Characters that had become known to everybody, the ordinary man and woman in the street, flowed from his pen, and two in particular stood out as belonging to the dozen immortals of the literature of all ages. Pickwick and Sam Weller stand side by side with Don Quixote and Sancho Panza, Tom Jones and Partridge, Parson Adams, and, strange juxtaposition but none the less true, Hamlet.

A tragedy in this house profoundly affected Dickens not only at the time, but for the remainder of his life. His wife's younger sister, Mary, who lived with them, died with terrible suddenness. The publication of *Pickwick* was delayed for two months, and Dickens removed for a change of scene to Hampstead, where John Forster first visited him, and there began the friendship between them which " remained unweakened until death came."

The Doughty Street house is now owned by the Dickens Fellowship and is their headquarters. It contains a library and museum and is open to visitors.

Not very far away is a wide district of London where, fifteen or sixteen years before *Pickwick* was written, Dickens lived with his parents, first at 141, Bayham Street, Camden Town, which he described to Forster as " a mean small tenement, with a wretched little back garden." His father, at this time, was beset with money troubles, and young Charles, then about twelve years old, suffered much of the unhappiness which he records in *Copperfield* when lodging with the Micawbers. An extension of the Hampstead General Hospital now occupies its site.

The great network of adjacent railway lines stretching out northward from King's Cross and St. Pancras, obliterated " Harmon's Dust Heaps," or " Boffin's Bower," and " Staggs's Gardens " where Susan Nipper took Florence Dombey on a surreptitious visit to Polly Toodle.

While the Dickens family lived in Bayham Street, Mr. John Dickens (the father of Charles) was arrested for debt and lodged in the Marshalsea prison. The home was broken up ; Mrs. Dickens went to live with her husband in the prison, and young Charles went into a lodging with a reduced old lady in Little College Street, Camden Town, who afterwards figured as Mrs. Pipchin in *Dombey and Son*. " My own exclusive breakfast, of a penny cottage loaf and a pennyworth of milk, I provided for myself. I kept another small loaf and a quarter of a pound of cheese on a particular shelf of a particular cupboard, to make my supper on when I came back at night. They made a hole in the six or seven shillings I know well, and I was out at the blacking warehouse all day and had to support myself upon that money all the week."

The foregoing is quoted from Forster, to whom it was related by Dickens, who afterwards transcribed it into *Copperfield* (XI). He was so wretched in this lodging, so lonely, that he begged his father, whom he saw in the Marshalsea every Sunday, to allow him to live near at hand ; so a lodging was found for him in Lant Street, quite near the prison, of which more hereafter.

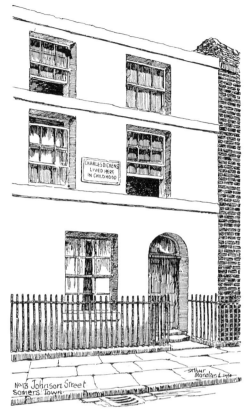

N°13 Johnson Street
Somers Town

On his release from the Marshalsea, Mr. Dickens went to live at No. 29 (now No. 13), Johnson Street, Somers Town. The family circumstances showed some improvement, but young Charles still worked at the blacking factory, walking there every morning, " with some cold hotchpotch in a basin tied up in a handkerchief for my dinner." With the doubtful exception of the house in Lant Street, this is the only house left in London associated with Dickens's childhood. It is now established as the "David Copperfield Library for Children."

A somewhat long stretch past St. Pancras and down Pentonville Road to the Angel, Dickens country, all of it ; but everything that could be identified has been destroyed. This brings us to City Road, where there remains, in all its dinginess, Windsor Terrace, immortalized as the location of Mr. Micawber's residence.

At the City Road end there is a crescent-shaped open space with a melancholy-looking drinking-fountain in the centre, which appears to have been placed there as a reminder of Mr. Micawber's ability to be cheerful under the most adverse circumstances. Standing by it and looking down the dismal length of Windsor Terrace, no one would be surprised to see the black tights, brown surtout and shirt-collar of that gentleman, progress down one of the flights of steps that lead from each front-door, casting a disdainful glance at the parlour window next door where the lady who lived there " exposed hard-bake for sale," and an apprehensive one opposite, where a sheriffs' officer resided.

Even so long ago as Mr. Micawber's day, nearly a hundred years since, Windsor Terrace had fallen from its once high estate. The houses are large and must, originally, have been the homes of City merchants, but they were then let out in tenements, as they appear to be now. In *David Copperfield* (XI) Mr. Micawber first meets David in the offices of Murdstone and Grinby, Mr. Murdstone having arranged for David to lodge with him. David was summoned to Mr. Quinion's office, and there saw " a stoutish, middle-aged person, in a brown surtout and black tights and shoes, with no more hair upon his head (which was a large one and very shining) than there is upon an egg, and with a very extensive face, which he turned full upon me. His clothes were shabby, but he had an imposing shirt-collar on. He carried a jaunty sort of stick, with a large pair of rusty tassels to it ; a quizzing glass hung outside his coat— for ornament, I afterwards found, as he very seldom looked through it, and couldn't see anything when he did." The introduction made and the object of his visit explained,

Mr. Micawber addressing David said, " ' My address is Windsor Terrace, City Road. I—in short,' said Mr. Micawber, with a genteel air and a burst of confidence, ' I live there.  Under the impression that your peregrinations in this metropolis have not yet been extensive, and, that you might have some difficulty in penetrating the arcana of the Modern Babylon in the direction of the City Road—in short,' said Mr. Micawber in another burst of confidence, ' that you might lose yourself—I shall be happy to call this evening, and instal you in the knowledge of the nearest way.' "

Dickens adapted Mr. Micawber's grandiloquent style of speech from his father's habit of using, on occasion, a similar form of address.  Other points of resemblance point to Mr. Dickens, Senior, as being the model for Micawber, who is, perhaps, the greatest of Dickens's comic characters.  He is so intensely human, so alive, such an object-lesson to those of us inclined to pessimism to try to cultivate its antidote. Micawber, like many of Dickens's characters, has added another word to the English language.

Windsor Terrace – City Road.

Arthur Moreland. '93.

43

# V

# The City

THE map shows Ludgate and what is now Farringdon Street as it was seven years before the date of *Pickwick Papers*. The Fleet Prison, with all its horrors, was still standing, and La Belle Sauvage an important stage-coach centre, with the Inn at the extreme top end of the long narrow yard.

The prisoners in the Fleet and other debtors' prisons were deprived of nothing except their liberty. A debtor was put into the prison and then left to look after himself; the Government treated him worse than a convicted felon, who was lodged, fed and clothed. The debtor had to feed himself, or starve, wear his own clothing, and, if he could not afford to pay for a bed, sleep anywhere and anyhow. They could buy their food in the prison, or obtain it from without; beer and wine were permitted, but spirits were, officially, prohibited, though with the connivance of the turnkeys there was no difficulty in getting any form of alcoholic drink. It needs no strain on the imagination to realize what dens of corruption and extortion these places were.

With reference to the supply of drink, the map shows on the lower boundary of the prison a small building, evidently a guard-house near to a gate, indicated by a thin

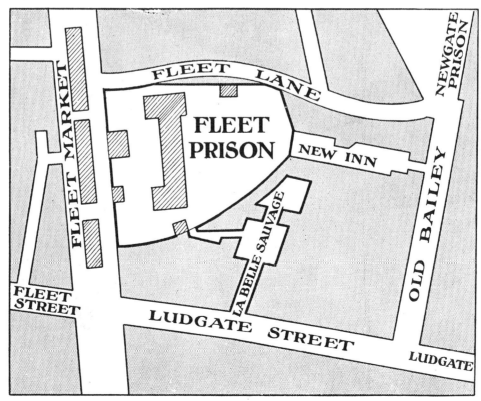

line, leading directly to La Belle Sauvage Yard. It is obvious that the inn did a roaring trade with the thirsty section of prisoners, when they' had money to spend.

That portion of *Pickwick Papers* describing Mr. Pickwick's imprisonment gives a vivid picture of the conditions obtaining in these places, and Dickens, at the outset of his career, struck the first blow towards the reform and subsequent abolition of this dreadful system. He was to follow with the exposure of other public abuses, and no writer of fiction ever succeeded in the achievement of so much reform, as often as not —as in the case of Mrs. Gamp and Mrs. Prig—under the guise of humour.

La Belle Sauvage Inn and Coaching House is mentioned. in 1453. The long yard was divided into two courts, the Inn being built round the inner court. The outer court, near Ludgate Hill, was entered through the present arch—the only remaining fragment of the original Belle Sauvage. The Inn was the London headquarters of Mr. Tony Weller. It was demolished in 1873 and it is appropriate that this book should be born on its site, Messrs. Cassell's premises practically following the lines of the old

Inn. As was a common practice before the establishment of regular theatres, plays were often performed in the yard. Wyatt's rebellion ended here ; unable to force Lud Gate, he rested in Belle Sauvage Yard, before attempting to retreat by fighting his way back to Temple Bar, where he was forced to surrender.

The business premises, and residence, of the " old-established firm of Anthony Chuzzlewit and Son," is described in Chapter XI as being " in a very narrow street somewhere behind the Post Office," that is, the old building, now pulled down, that stood on the east side of St. Martin le Grand.

" A dim, dirty, smoky, tumble-down, rotten old house it was." In order to complete its description,

La Belle Sauvage
Arthur Moreland.
'31

it is necessary to refer to that part of the story where Jonas Chuzzlewit is laying his plans to murder Tigg Montague, and is preparing to establish an alibi (Chapter XLVI). He tells his wife to put his supper " in the little off room below, and have the truckle-bed made. I shall sleep there to-night, and maybe to-morrow night, and if I can sleep all day to-morrow, so much the better, for I've got trouble to sleep off, if I can. Keep the house quiet, and don't call me. Mind ! Don't call me. Don't let anybody call me. Let me lie there." When the room was ready Jonas went down to it and put his boots outside the door, that is, the door inside the house, communicating with this little detached room, which was " on the ground floor, at the back of the house. It was lighted by a dirty skylight, and had a door opening into a narrow covered passage or blind-alley, with an outlet in a neighbouring street. The ground on which this chamber was built had, at one time, not within his recollection, been a yard ; and had been converted to its present purpose for use as an office. . . . It was a blotched, stained, mouldering room, like a vault ; and there were water-pipes running through it, which at unexpected times in the night, clicked and gurgled suddenly, as if they were choking."

Jonas's preparations are then described. He had taken his portmanteau into the room, and from it he took clothes and boots such as a countryman, or farm labourer, would wear. He dressed himself in them, tumbled the bed to give it the appearance of having been slept in, oiled the lock of the outer door, rusty from long disuse, and sat on the bed with the key in his hand, waiting. The ringers were practising in a neighbouring church—St. Vedast's churchyard wall forms one side of the passage —and the sound of the bells maddened him. The story of the murder and the tracking of the murderer is not what we are concerned with, but with the identification of the house, and the room in which Jonas was lurking.

First, the front of the house in Foster Lane. It has recently been covered with stucco and painted, and, in consequence, does not seem to merit the description of " rotten and tumble-down." It was much more convincing before the bricks were covered. The shop-front may, or may not, be a comparatively modern addition— but there is no doubt about the antiquity of the house. At the latest it dates from just after the Great Fire and may be one of the few survivors. It is when we go up Priest's Court and compare what is there with Dickens's detailed description that all reason for doubt disappears. The room was palpably added to the house long after it was originally built. The door opens into the " narrow covered passage or blind-alley " —the passage is a blind-alley with " its outlet in the neighbouring street." Further evidence is provided by the complicated system of water-pipes all converging upon a main pipe sunk into the wall of the room, and which would be liable to " click and gurgle as if they were choking." Every detail stands to-day exactly as it is described, and there can be no doubt but that it is the house where one of the most loathsome villains ever depicted planned his wickedness and, finally, met his fate.

The old houses on the west side of Foster Lane were pulled down many years ago, and with them, the one from which Nadgett kept his patient watch. He saw Jonas

No 5 Foster Lane
Cheapside

Arthur Moreland 1931

Priest's Court
5 Foster Lane

Arthur
Moreland.
1931

leave, and following him, lost him as he travelled westward. He went back to his window, and waited until Jonas came creeping back, to come out again carrying a bundle. The rest of the story is told later on.

Dickens's sense of humour at once responded to humbug, especially that variety assumed by professional men, doctors, lawyers, and, lower down the scale, the hired solemnity of the undertaker. The description of the funeral of old Anthony Chuzzlewit (Chap. XIX), with its extraordinary mixture of grimness and comedy, is a brilliant example. "At length the day of the funeral, pious and truthful ceremony that it was, arrived. Mr. Mould [the undertaker], with a glass of generous port between his eye and the light, leaned against the desk in the little glass office with his gold watch in his unoccupied hand, and conversed with Mrs. Gamp ; two mutes were at the house-door, looking as mournful as could be reasonably expected of men with such a thriving job in hand."

As the funeral was about to start Mr. Mould addressed his foreman : " Ah, what a man he was ! Ah, Tacker, Tacker, what a man he was !" Immediately after, Mr. Tacker, " who, from his great experience in the performance of funerals, would have made an excellent pantomime actor, winked at Mrs. Gamp without at all disturbing the gravity of his countenance." The funeral over, the chapter ends with this contrast:

" The hearse, after standing for a long time at the door of a roystering public-house, repaired to its stable with the feathers inside and twelve red-nosed undertakers on the roof, each holding on by a dingy peg, to which, in times of state, a waving plume was fitted." " The gates [of the churchyard] were closed ; the night was dark and wet ; and the rain fell silently among the stagnant weeds and nettles. One new mound was there which had not been last night. Time, burrowing like a mole underground, had marked his track by throwing up another heap of earth. And that was all."

There is more about Mr. Mould in Chapter XXV. His establishment is situated within the ward of Cheap ; and his little back sitting-room, over the little counting-house behind the shop, overlooked a churchyard, small and shady. Mr. Mould is in the bosom of his family. " From the distant shop a pleasant sound arose of coffin-making with a low melodious hammer." Tacker, the foreman, puts his head in at the door and asks Mr. Mould whether he " would be inclined to take a walking one of two, with the plain wood and a tin plate." Mr. Mould indignantly refuses, but on being informed that the deceased is the Beadle's son-in-law, consents on condition that the Beadle follows " in his cocked hat—not else."

Mrs. Gamp also calls and her constitutional weakness is delicately indicated by the statement that at the moment of her appearance, " a peculiar fragrance was borne upon the breeze, as if a passing fairy had hiccoughed, and had previously been to a wine-vaults." The churchyard is St. Olave's, Old Jewry.

The church is now an institute for young people working in the City. Mr. Mould's shop would be in Old Jewry alongside the churchyard which, at that time, was open to the street.

" Mr. Pickwick and Sam took up their present abode in very good, old-fashioned,

St Olave's Churchyard
Old Jewry

arthur
Moreland
1931

50

and comfortable quarters : to wit, the George and Vulture Tavern and Hotel, George Yard, Lombard-Street " (*Pickwick*, Chap. XXVI).

Nowadays George Yard is little more than a narrow passage and the crowded office buildings along it have all but obliterated this famous old tavern ; there being nothing visible from George Yard but a narrow corner strip from ground to roof. In Chapter XXXI Mr. Jackson, clerk to Messrs. Dodson and Fogg, calls and inquires at the bar for Mr. Pickwick. Mr. Jackson, instead of waiting for the waiter to return from upstairs, follows him into Mr. Pickwick's private room, where Mr. Pickwick is sitting with Mr. Snodgrass, Mr. Tupman and Mr. Winkle, who are each invested with a slip of paper and one shilling by Mr. Jackson.

Mr. Pickwick returned to the George and Vulture on his release from the Fleet. Mr. Winkle also stayed there after his marriage to Arabella Allen, and here Mr. Winkle, Senior, unexpectedly arrived (Chapter LVI) and was reconciled to his son and daughter-in-law. Mr. Weller, Senior, had also been one of Mr. Pickwick's visitors, on the same

The George & Vulture

day, leaving with Mr. Pickwick, much to that gentleman's astonishment, the whole of his realized capital in a bulky wallet.

Another London churchyard, St. Peter upon Cornhill, was the scene of the meeting of Bradley Headstone and Lizzie Hexam in *Our Mutual Friend* (XV), where it is related that Headstone, with Lizzie's brother, Charlie, was waiting in Leadenhall Street, spying eastward for Lizzie. As she came in sight they went forward to meet her, and Charlie, with the purpose of gaining for Headstone the opportunity to say what was in his mind, drew attention to "a paved court by a church."

The churchyard is described as "a paved square court, with a raised bank of earth about breast high, in the middle, enclosed by iron rails. Here, conveniently and healthfully elevated above the level of the living, were the dead, and the tombstones ; some of the latter droopingly inclined from the perpendicular, as if they were ashamed of the lies they told." At this period many people lived, were born, and ultimately died within the City boundary ; and it was the custom to bury them either inside the church or in the churchyard. There would not be one City churchyard to which this description would not apply. Nowadays, they form trim and shady resting-places during the luncheon hour for City workers.

Charlie Hexam made an appeal, a selfish appeal, to his sister to listen favourably to Bradley Headstone, and left them together. A scene followed during which Bradley, half-crazed with passion and jealousy, laid his hand on a piece of the coping forming the burial-ground enclosure and wrenched it so that the powdered mortar from under the stone rattled on the pavement.

This interview, fruitless as it was for Bradley Headstone, set his feet on the path that was to end in attempted murder.

St. Olave's Hart Street.
Gateway in Seething Lane.
Arthur Moreland 1921

The church of St. Olave, Hart Street, is one of the few to escape that stood in the path of the Great Fire. It is famous as the parish church of Samuel Pepys, his pew being in a gallery on the south side of the church, the entrance to which was by an outside stairway, the marks of which may still be seen on the wall of the church. On the north side of the chancel is a portrait bust of Mrs. Pepys, who died in 1669 and is buried in the vault below the Altar, where Pepys himself was placed when he died, in 1703.

The churchyard was used for burials during the Great Plague, this fact probably influencing the artist who designed the gate and which Dickens describes in *The Uncommercial Traveller* in the chapter entitled "The City of the Absent."

Churchyard of St Peter-on-Cornhill.

Arthur
Moreland.
1931

" One of my best beloved churchyards I call Saint Ghastly Grim ; touching what men in general call it, I have no information.   It lies in the heart of the City and the Blackwall Railway shrieks at it daily.   It is a small churchyard, with a ferocious strong spiked iron gate, like a jail.   This gate is ornamented with skulls and crossbones, larger than life, wrought in stone ; but it likewise came into the mind of Saint Ghastly Grim, that to stick iron spikes atop of the stone skulls, as though they were impaled, would be a pleasant device.   Therefore the skulls grin aloft horribly, thrust through and through with iron spears."

The gate is at the south-east corner of the churchyard in Seething Lane.

Aldgate Pump stands at the junction of Leadenhall Street and Fenchurch Street with Aldgate.   It is on the site of a well dedicated to St. Michael and has been in use for hundreds of years.   On several occasions Mr. Toots, unable to bear the sight of

Aldgate Pump.

Arthur Moreland
'31

Walter Gay and Florence Dombey as lovers, would suddenly leave the little back parlour behind the Wooden Midshipman and walk either to the Royal Exchange, ostensibly to time his watch, or to Aldgate Pump (*Dombey and Son,* LV).

Old Sol Gills, the original owner of the Wooden Midshipman, had his shop on the north side of Leadenhall Street.   About eighty years ago this business and two other ships' instrument makers amalgamated ;   the present proprietors of the Midshipman are Messrs. Ismay Laurie, Norie and Wilson, 123, Minories, where he is still to be seen inside the shop.   The firm has refused many tempting offers for him, especially from America.

The Six Jolly Fellowship Porters Tavern is in Narrow Street, Limehouse.   The way to it is so devious that simple directions will not be out of place.   The best way is a No. 15 omnibus from Charing Cross, which passes along Aldgate, to Limehouse Church. Three Colt Street, at the east end of the church, brings you to Narrow Street, and The Grapes Inn, for that is its name, is on the left-hand side after about eight minutes' walk.   It is easy to miss, being, on the side facing the street, small and flat-fronted.

It is first mentioned in *Our Mutual Friend* (III) on the night of the recovery of the drowned body of the supposed John Harmon.   The inquest was held there, in the upper room, overlooking Limehouse Reach.   It is an old house, probably three hundred years old, with great oak beams as hard as steel.

In Chapter VI there is a full description of the house.   " Externally, it was a narrow, lopsided, wooden jumble of corpulent windows heaped one upon another as you might heap as many toppling oranges, with a crazy wooden verandah impending over the water.   This description applies to the river frontage of the Six Jolly Fellowship Porters. The back of the establishment, though the chief entrance was there, so contracted that it merely represented, in its connexion with the front, the handle of a flat-iron set upright at its broadest end.

" The bar of the Six Jolly Fellowship Porters was a bar to soften the human breast. The available space in it was not much larger than a hackney-coach ; but no one could have wished the bar bigger, that space was so girt in by corpulent little casks, and by cordial-bottles radiant with fictitious grapes in bunches. . . . The landlady's own small table in a snug corner by the fire, with the cloth everlastingly laid.

" This haven was divided from the rough world by a glass partition and a half-door.

" For the rest, both the tap and the parlour of the Six Jolly Fellowship Porters gave upon the river, and had red curtains, matching the noses of the regular customers."

The identity of the Six Jolly Fellowship Porters with the Grapes Inn is certain. Its original name was The Bunch of Grapes, and the present proprietor remembers bottles being in the bar, with bunches of grapes moulded in the glass. Here is an instance of Dickens's powers of observation. The bar, " not much larger than a hackney-coach," was enlarged some years ago ; the front of the house being pulled down and rebuilt further out. A wooden beam across the ceiling, about four feet from the doorway,

The Grapes Inn.
The Upper Room.

Arthur
Moreland.
1931

indicates the size of the room in its original state.  The glass partition, but no longer with a half-door, is there, and beyond it is Miss Abbey Potterson's little snuggery.  The house should be visited at low tide, otherwise it is impossible to go further than " the wooden verandah."

The Grapes Inn.
The little room
behind the Bar

Arthur
Moreland.
'24

The Grapes Inn
Limehouse

Arthur
Moreland.
1931

57

# VI

# Southwark

BOROUGH HIGH STREET is the London end of the old Dover Road, really old, for it has seen two thousand years, and it is only within the present century that its original line has been interfered with by the making of by-passes to cut off corners and to meet, generally, the needs of the re-born road traffic. The history of this road is the history of England ; first the Roman legions, the Crusaders, the triumphant return of Edward from Crecy and Henry from Agincourt, Chaucer's Canterbury pilgrims, Charles II at the Restoration, it has seen them all. As it mounts Blackheath it has been decorated with gibbets bearing the remains of highwaymen swinging in loose iron cages.

"There are milestones on the Dover Road," as that extraordinary female in *Little Dorrit*, Mr. F.'s Aunt, observed apropos of nothing in particular, but whenever she did interject the information it always seemed to make everybody uncomfortable. Dickens had been along it many times, in stage-coach, post-chaise and on foot, for he is able to describe little David Copperfield's weary journey of six days from London to Dover.

The railways have robbed Borough High Street of most of its picturesqueness. In the days of the stage-coach, old galleried inns—at least four—were within a short distance of one another. The Spur, Queen's Head, White Hart and the George, of which only a portion of the last-named remains and has recently been scheduled as "an historic building."

For our present purpose it is best to reach Southwark by way of London Bridge, where the Monument, designed by Wren and commemorating the Great Fire, is erected. The Dickens student, on seeing it, immediately thinks of Todgers's Boarding Establishment. Chapter IX of *Martin Chuzzlewit* opens with a description of Todgers's and its immediate neighbourhood. On a bright day, "the shadow of the Monument fell across it," which confines exploration to a comparatively limited half-circle. Nowadays, it is, of course, hopeless to find even the place where it may have stood, but twenty-five years ago, you could, to a certain extent, "grope your way through lanes and bye-ways, court-yards and passages," to be "stopped by a dead wall or an iron railing."

Dickens must have known it, for, with his customary exactness, he describes it without, within and on the roof which had "a sort of terrace with posts and fragments of rotten lines, once intended to dry clothes upon ; and two or three tea-chests, full of earth, with forgotten plants in them, like old walking-sticks." Though many surmises have been made, Todgers's has never been found and it is probable that it was pulled down soon after Dickens, engaged on his usual search, decided upon it as being suitable for his purpose.

Both flights of steps on the western side of London Bridge are connected with a murder. Down the flight on the Middlesex side of the river, Jonas Chuzzlewit went to sink the bundle containing the clothes in which he had disguised himself when he set out to murder Tigg Montague. Mr. Nadgett (Chap. LI) relates what he saw from his hiding-place in the house opposite to 5, Foster Lane. " ' I kept at the window all day. I think I never closed my eyes. At night, I saw him come out with a bundle. I followed him again. He went down the steps at London Bridge, and sunk it in the river.' " Nadgett went to the police, and the bundle of clothes, " stained with clay and spotted with blood," was fished out.

The steps at the southern end of the bridge is where Nancy in *Oliver Twist* (XLVI) took Mr. Brownlow and Rose Maylie, so that, as she thought, she might speak to them without being seen. " ' Not here,' she said ; ' I'm afraid to speak to you here. Come away—out of the public road—down the steps yonder ! ' " Noah Claypole had followed her, and, overhearing her, hurried away and stole down the steps ahead of them.

Dickens's description of the steps is accurate in every detail. " The steps to which the girl had pointed, were those which, on the Surrey bank, and on the same side of

Steps at S.W. end of
London Bridge

Arthur
Moreland.
1931

the bridge as St. Saviour's Church [now Southwark Cathedral], form landing stairs from the river.   These stairs are a part of the bridge : they consist of three flights. Just below the end of the second, going down, the stone wall on the left terminates in an ornamental pilaster facing towards the Thames.   At this point the lower steps widen : so that a person turning that angle of the wall, is necessarily unseen by any others on the stairs who chance to be above him, if only a step.   The countryman [Claypole] looked hastily round, when he reached this point ; and, as there seemed no better place of concealment, and, the tide being out, there was plenty of room, he slipped aside, with his back to the pilaster, and there waited : pretty certain that they would come no lower, and that even if he could not hear what was said, he could follow them again with safety."

Noah Claypole overheard the conversation between Mr. Brownlow, Rose Maylie and Nancy.   When they had gone, he hurried away and made for Fagin's house.   The following chapter tells the sequel.   Fagin, convinced that Nancy intends to betray him and the rest of the gang, tells Sikes what he has heard from Claypole, and Sikes murders Nancy.   This chapter is one of those read by Dickens when he gave his series of public readings.

Proceeding towards Borough High Street we pass the Borough Market on the right. The door on the steps of which Mr. Ben Allen spent the night after the bachelor party in Lant Street, *Pickwick* (XXXII), knocking double knocks at intervals, being under the impression that he lived there, was demolished and the market set further back when the railway-bridge was built.

Further down the street, on the east side, is the entrance to George Yard and the George Inn Hotel.   This is the only remaining galleried inn left in London, though in the stage-coach days there were many others.

Originally the inn occupied a square surrounding the yard, of which only the south side remains.   The coach entrance is behind the wooden gate on the right as you enter, the archway leading from the street being demolished ; finally the whole street front was replaced by other buildings, so that no portion of the old  house now faces the street.

The White Hart, where Sam Weller was boots, stood a few doors further north on the same side.   It has completely disappeared, with not even a modern gin-palace to mark the spot.   The suggestion has been advanced that Dickens had the George in his mind when he wrote White Hart in *Pickwick* (X), describing Mr. Pickwick's arrival there after a headlong all-night ride in a post-chaise from Dingley Dell, with Mr. Wardle, in pursuit of Jingle and Miss Rachael Wardle.   There is no reason why he should have meant the George, for the White Hart was a similar house, almost if not quite as important as the George, and, like it, was galleried round two sides of its square.   Except for a mere mention in *Little Dorrit*, the George is not a Dickens land-mark, beyond the fact that he knew it, and it is on record that he visited it on more than one occasion.

We are now in that part of the Borough which figures in *Little Dorrit*.   Up the High Street, a few yards before reaching the street separating you from St. George's

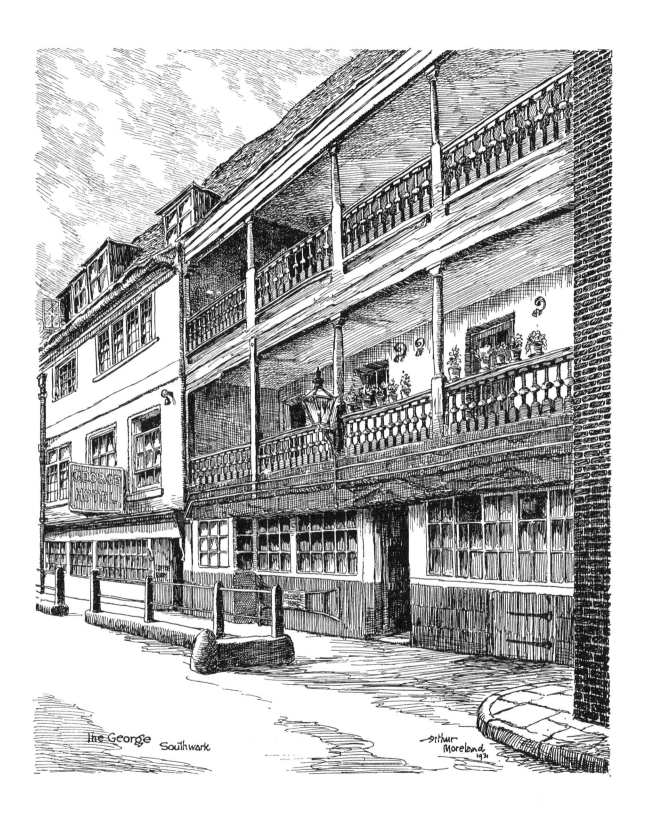

The George Southwark

Arthur Moreland
1931

Marshalsea Place
Southwark.

Arthur
Moreland
1931

Church, a low arched opening on the left, Angel Place, leads to Marshalsea Place, thus described in the Preface to *Little Dorrit*. "Some of mý readers may have an interest in being informed whether or no any portions of the Marshalsea Prison are yet standing. I, myself, did not know until I was approaching the end of this story, when I went to look. I found the outer front courtyard, often mentioned here, metamorphosed into a butter-shop ; and I then almost gave up every brick of the jail as lost. Wandering, however, down a certain adjacent Angel Court [leading to Bermondsey],

I came to Marshalsea Place, the houses in which I recognized, not only as the great block of the former prison, but as preserving the rooms that arose in my mind's eye when I became Little Dorrit's biographer. . . . Whosoever goes into Marshalsea Place, will find his feet on the very paving-stones of the extinct Marshalsea Jail ; will see its narrow yard, very little altered if at all, will look upon the rooms in which the debtors lived ; and will stand among the crowding ghosts of many miserable years."

By going straight on and making two succeeding turns to the right, you will have walked round the site of the prison. The massive wall on your right, for part of the way, is, with what has been described, the only remaining relic of these Debtors' Prisons. Dickens's father was confined here in 1824-25.

Little Dorrit's Garret.
Marshalsea Prison

arthur moreland

The original Marshalsea was further north, near Newcomen Street, and was a prison as far back as 1327. Bishop Bonner was a prisoner and died there in Elizabeth's time, being buried in St. George's Church, the predecessor of the present church. The Marshalsea of Dickens appears to have been an extension of the older prison.

An iron gate in some high railings opposite the north side of the church leads to " Little Dorrit's Garden," a pleasant open space formed of what was part of St. George's churchyard and the inner court of the prison, but where one ends and the other begins it is impossible to say. On the left are the old prison buildings, and a garret window at the southern end is pointed out as Little Dorrit's room. There is quite a considerable portion of the prison to be seen, notably two heavily barred windows.

It was in the vestry at the west end of St. George's Church that Little Dorrit and Maggy, returning from what they looked upon as " a party " at Arthur Clennam's house, found themselves locked out. The prison gate was locked at a fixed time and no one could either leave or enter after that hour. They were preparing to pass the night as best they could, when Little Dorrit saw lights in the church. The sexton was, as he explained, kept late by the painters and he had a fire in the vestry. He brought them in, stirred the vestry fire, got some cushions out of the church, and spread them before the fire (Chap. XIV). He knew Little Dorrit quite well as an inmate of the prison, and taking a particular volume from the shelves of registers, he said, " ' Here you'll find yourself as large as life. " Amy, daughter of William and Fanny Dorrit. Born, Marshalsea Prison, Parish of St. George." And we tell people that you've lived there, without so much as a day's or a night's absence, ever since. Is it true ? '

" ' Quite true, till last night.' "

There are many similar entries in the registers, and it reveals the system of imprisonment for debt in all

Little Dorrit's Vestry
St. George's Church

Arthur
Moreland.
1931

St Georges —
Church
Southwark

Arthur Moreland 1931

its horror.   It was life sentence for many ;   for the other department of the registers which record the end of life as well as the beginning, contains sufficient evidence to prove that these unfortunate people were, even if ill, still prisoners to live or die as the case might be.

Little Dorrit and Maggy passed a comfortable night and returned " home " directly the gate was unlocked.

St. George's Church stands on the site of a church dating from the twelfth century, the present building being erected in 1736.   It was the parish church of both the Marshalsea and the King's Bench prisons, and the burial-place for prisoners who died in either place.   Many of the old gravestones to be seen in " Little Dorrit's Garden " may be those of some long-forgotten debtor.   Little Dorrit, as well as being baptized, was also married here to Arthur Clennam (Chap. LXX).

Lant Street is about one hundred yards further south on the opposite side of the street.   Introducing Lant Street in *Pickwick* (XXXII), Dickens says, " If a man wished to abstract himself from the world ;   to remove himself from within the reach of tempta- tion ;   to place himself beyond the possibility of any inducement to look out of the window ;   he should by all means go to Lant Street."

An observant visitor will notice that since the above was written, Lant Street has

Lant Street
Southwark

seen little or no change in its outward appear- ance ; the houses are nearly a hundred years older, but it has an odd air about it that it will look very much the same at the end of still another century.

David Copperfield (Chap. XI) relates that he went to the King's Bench Prison to see Mr. and Mrs. Micawber. This is autobiographi- cal, for it was Dickens himself, then twelve years old, who made his regular Sunday visit to his parents, though not to the King's Bench prison, but the Mar- shalsea. He had been placed in lodgings in Little College Street,

Camden Town (see page 40). The Micawber home being broken up, David says that a lodging was found for him in the neighbourhood, while " the Orfling " was likewise accommodated in a room not far away. The Orfling was Mrs. Micawber's little servant; her prototype was Mrs. Dickens's maid, who had been brought from Chatham. When Mrs. Dickens joined her husband in the prison the Orfling went with her; she did not sleep in the prison, however, but in a lodging in Lant Street. Young Charles, miserable and lonely in his lodgings, appealed to his father to provide for him nearer to the prison, and a back attic in the same house in Lant Street was found for him, which, to his great delight, looked over a timber-yard.

Some distance up the left-hand side of Lant Street several of the old houses and a public-house were pulled down for the erection of a National School, and it is supposed that it was in one of these houses that young Dickens and the Orfling were lodged. There is little, if any, more evidence for this than for the claim of another house, shown

Tavern in Lant Street

in the drawing as the second door from the open gate of the yard behind the houses which may, in its time, have been the timber-yard.

Whichever house it was, Dickens, little more than twelve years later, when writing *Pickwick*, placed Mr. Bob Sawyer, a medical student at Guy's Hospital, in lodgings in Lant Street with the redoubtable Mrs. Raddle as his landlady. But she was not the landlady that Dickens knew, for both she and her husband were elderly people, and were very kind to their young lodger. They afterwards lived again as the Garland family in *The Old Curiosity Shop*. There is no doubt that while living in Lant Street Dickens saw the originals of Mr. and Mrs. Raddle. They may have lived next door, and it is they who contribute the main interest to this street.

In *Pickwick* (XXXII) is the account of Bob Sawyer's bachelor party, at which Mr. Pickwick, Mr. Snodgrass and Mr. Winkle were among the guests. Before the party Mrs. Raddle applies for arrears of rent, but Mr. Sawyer has been " disappointed in the City." Immediately on receipt of this information, Mrs. Raddle embarks upon a long vituperative oration, in the course of which she asks, " Do you suppose a hard-working and industrious woman as has lived in this street for twenty year (ten year over the way, and nine year and three-quarter in this very house)"—from which it will be seen that Mrs. Raddle had lived in both houses, and therefore the chance of the house still standing being the one we would wish it to be is, at the least, reasonable.

This house is only a few yards from High Street, and Mr. Sawyer had purchased the beef and ham " from a German-sausage shop round the corner." There are no shops in or near Lant Street, except in Borough High Street, and the words, " round the corner," clearly indicate that High Street was close at hand. " Round the corner " from where the alternative house stood, is three or four minutes' walk as against one minute.

Upon which house is which, depends the identity of the public-house where Mr. Sawyer borrowed the glasses. " The landlady's glasses were little thin blown-glass tumblers, and those which had been borrowed from the public-house were great, dropsical, bloated articles, each supported on a huge gouty leg."

The evidence in favour of the existing house is so strong, that a drawing of the near-by public-house has been included. Its name, The Gladstone, might suggest that it is not, as a public-house, of sufficient age, for one hundred years ago that great statesman had not attained to that eminence and widespread popularity that would, regardless of consequences, lead a brewer or a licensed victualler to name a public-house after him. The house was standing, and had been devoted to its present purpose for many years before Mr. Gladstone was born, and one is inclined to the belief that, at some time or another, some enthusiastic admirer changed its name. That argument's vulnerable point is in the fact that if there was a section of the community to which that great man's popularity did not extend, it was " the Trade."

St. George's Circus, Blackfriars Road, is where David Copperfield, at the outset of his long walk to Dover, met a young man with a donkey-cart, standing near the Obelisk in the Blackfriars Road (Chap. XII). The Obelisk was removed some years ago to

St George's Circus
and Surrey Theatre

Arthur
Moreland
1931

be substituted by an over-ornate clock tower, and placed within the railings of what was, until recently, the Bethlehem Hospital, and is now the Geraldine Harmsworth Park, no longer telling the truth as to the distance from where it stands to London Bridge.

David wished to transport his box from his lodging to the booking-office, and seeing " a long-legged young man with a very little empty donkey-cart standing near the Obelisk, in the Blackfriars Road, whose eye I caught as I was going by, and who, addressing me as ' Sixpenn'orth o' bad ha'pence,' hoped ' I should know him again to swear to '—in allusion, I have no doubt, to my staring at him.

26 Newman Street

Arthur
Moreland
1931

I stopped to assure him that I had not done so in bad manners, but uncertain whether he might or might not like a job.

" ' Wot job ? ' said the long-legged young man.

" ' To move a box,' I answered.

" ' Wot box ? ' said the long-legged young man.

" I told him mine, which was down that street there, and which I wanted him to take to the Dover coach-office for sixpence.

" ' Done with you for a tanner ! ' said the long-legged young man."

The end of this incident was that David was robbed of his box and a half-guinea that he had borrowed from Peggotty, all the money he had, except a few pence. The story of his long walk is another matter, but it may be noted that it is fiction and not autobiography. Dickens spent his boyhood in London and gained his success entirely by his own efforts, for there was no Betsey Trotwood, nor anyone like her, among his relatives.

The Surrey Theatre, on the left, is the third to stand on this site, and was built in 1865. Its predecessor was where Fanny Dorrit was a dancer, her uncle Frederick being a clarionet player in the orchestra.

In the same theatre Nicholas Nickleby's actor friend, Vincent Crummles, made "positively his last appearance." In *Nickleby* (XLVIII) Nicholas was returning from one of many missions to Madeline.Bray, who was living with her father within the Rules of the King's Bench, and his way back to the City was walking along Blackfriars Road. Worried and anxious as to the fate of Madeline, "Nicholas found himself poring with the utmost interest over a large play-bill hanging outside a Minor Theatre which he had to pass on his way home, and reading the list of actors and actresses who had promised to do honour to some approaching benefit . . . he glanced at the top of the bill . . . and there saw announced, in large letters with a large space between each of them, pearance of Mr. Vincent 'Positively the last ap-Celebrity.' " Nicholas Crummles of Provincial was rapturously received sent in his name, and Crummles, Master by Mr. Crummles, Mrs. Crummles, and the In- Crummles, Master Percy fant Phenomenon.

The Golden Dog,
Blackfriars Rd.

At the corner of Blackfriars Road and Union Street—formerly Charlotte Street—is The Golden Dog over the shop-front of Messrs. J. W. Cunningham & Co. In the first chapter of Forster's *Life*, Dickens relates to Forster that his " usual way home was over Blackfriars Bridge, and down that turning in Blackfriars Road which has Rowland Hill's Chapel [now The Ring] on one side, and the likeness of a golden dog licking a golden pot on the other." This particular sign dates from 1533 and was placed in its present position when the business was established in 1783.[1]

Newman Street, Oxford Street, may be visited at any convenient time. There is a connexion with *Bleak House* at No. 26, for here was Mr. Turveydrop's Dancing Academy. It is described (XIV) as " a sufficiently dingy house at the corner of an archway," the dancing academy being " built out into a mews at the back." The shop-window is a modern addition.

[1] Since the above was written this sign has been removed and sold.

## VII

## Highgate and Hampstead

THE steep hill by which you approach Highgate Village is largely responsible for the preservation of much of its old-world atmosphere. Modern progress demands speed and hills are to be avoided. Thus, the housebreaker has paused at the foot of the hill and has decided to keep to the level.

There is much about this part of Highgate in *David Copperfield*. Dr. Strong, David's old schoolmaster at Canterbury, lived here after his retirement, as did David himself after his marriage to Dora, while his aunt, Betsey Trotwood, lived close by. Mrs. Steerforth was also a resident at Highgate.

8 North Hill
Highgate Village.

Old Cottages on North Hill
Highgate Village

Dickens often went to Highgate Village to visit his friend Charles Mathews, the actor, who lived in a pleasant detached house on North Hill, No. 8, just such a house as Dr. Strong would have chosen, and there is little doubt that when Dickens needed a home for David's old schoolmaster, where he could continue his work on the Dictionary, he told his friend that Dr. Strong was going to live at No. 8, North Hill.

Almost immediately opposite this house is a row of old cottages with long gardens in front. The cottage at Highgate in which David and Dora lived had a garden, as also had the one close by in which Miss Trotwood lived. There is no specific description, except that David and Dora's home was small and pretty, but there is little doubt that two of these cottages were made to serve the required purpose.

Here began that extraordinary housekeeping (XLIV). "We had a servant," says David. "She kept house for us. I have still a latent belief that she must have been Mrs. Crupp's daughter in disguise. We had such a time of it with Mary Anne. She had a cousin in the Life Guards, with such long legs that he looked like the afternoon shadow of somebody else. He made the cottage smaller than it need have been by being so very much out of proportion to it." After Mary Anne there was an interval of Mrs. Kidgerbury, " the oldest inhabitant of Kentish Town, I believe, who went out charing, but was too feeble to execute her conceptions of that art—we found another treasure, who generally made a point of falling either up or down the kitchen stairs with the tray, and almost plunged into parlour, as into a bath, with the tea-things. She was succeeded (with intervals of Mrs. Kidgerbury) by a long line of Incapables ; terminating in a young person of genteel appearance, who went to Greenwich Fair in Dora's bonnet."

When David came to Highgate to find Dr. Strong, he says—" It was not in that part of Highgate where Mrs. Steerforth lived, but quite on the opposite side of the little town.   When I had made this discovery, I went back, . . . to a lane by Mrs. Steerforth's, and looked over the corner of the garden wall " (XXXVI).   This gives a distinct clue, for to get from North Hill to Mrs. Steerforth's house in South Grove, he would, having already passed it, have to turn back.

South Grove  to  this day is little more than a lane, and the Old Hall, a fine old house, stands exactly as described (Chap. XIX) when David says, " from the windows

The Old Hall
Highgate Village

The Spaniards
Hampstead.

of my room I saw all London lying in the distance like a great vapour," which is exactly the view from the back of the house. A few lines further on (XXXVI) surmise becomes certainty, for we read, " The church with the slender spire, that stands on the top of the hill now, was not there then to tell me the time. An old red-brick mansion, used as a school, was in its place." The " church with the slender spire " is next to the Old Hall, and stands on the site of an old house that was pulled down when the church was built.

The road from Highgate to Hampstead runs past Ken Wood and Ken Wood house, and a little further on is The Spaniards Inn. Dickens was very fond of Hampstead Heath and he knew The Spaniards well. Though it is not mentioned in *Barnaby Rudge*, the house has a connexion with the Gordon rioters who stopped there on their way to wreck Lord Mansfield's house in Caen (Ken) Wood. The landlord delayed them with supplies of drink, while he sent a messenger for help. Troops arrived and dispersed the rioters and some of the muskets they left behind are still preserved in the house. The inn, and the tea-garden at the back of the house, was the scene of the famous tea-party in *Pickwick* (XLVI). Mrs. Bardell and her son, Tommy Bardell, Mr. and Mrs. Raddle, Mrs. Cluppins (who was also Mrs. Raddle's sister), Mrs. Sanders, and Mrs. Rogers, who has succeeded Mr. Pickwick as Mrs. Bardell's lodger, formed the merry company round the tea-table in The Spaniards garden.

Mrs. Bardell, in virtue of her broken heart, owing to the contumacy of Mr. Pickwick, at that moment in the Fleet, was regarded as the most important person in the company, but it is round the unfortunate Mr. Raddle that the interest revolves. Earlier in the day, with his wife and sister-in-law, he had stepped into trouble, owing to the cabriolet in which the ladies wished to arrive at Mrs. Bardell's house in Goswell Street, "like real carriage folk," stopping at the wrong door. A subsequent altercation between the cabman and Mrs. Raddle, in regard to the fare, resulting in a victory for the cabman, Mrs. Raddle was led into the house tottering, all the blame for both incidents being heaped upon Raddle, who was requested to adjourn to the back-yard, out of his wife's sight, until she had recovered.

Arriving at The Spaniards, Raddle immediately, so to speak, blotted his copybook again, bringing Mrs. Raddle to the verge of a relapse by ordering tea for seven, whereas, as all the ladies remarked, "what could have been easier for Tommy to have drunk out of anybody's cup, when the waiter wasn't looking : which would have saved one head of tea." The conversation turned on the pleasantness of the country and Raddle, plucking up a little cheerfulness, plunged head over heels into disaster.

" ' For lone people,' observed Mr. Raddle, ' as have got nobody to care for them, or take care of them, or as have been hurt in their mind, or that kind of thing, the country is all very well. The country for a wounded spirit, they say.'

" Mrs. Bardell burst into tears, and requested to be led from the table instantly · upon which the affectionate child began to cry too, most dismally.

" ' Would anybody believe, ma'am,' exclaimed Mrs. Raddle, turning fiercely to the first-floor lodger, ' that a woman could be married to such an unmanly creetur, which can tamper with a woman's feelings, as he does, every hour in the day, ma'am ? ' "

Mr. Raddle's protestations of innocence were swept aside and Mrs. Rogers, busy with the smelling-bottle, recommended his retirement. This was seconded and carried unanimously, and Raddle quietly retired to a remote part of the garden.

At this moment a hackney-coach stopped at the garden-gate, and Mr. Jackson, of Dodson and Fogg's, stepped out. The suggestion was made that Mr. Pickwick might have paid the damages. Mr. Jackson, who was accompanied by a shabby man in black leggings, apologized for intruding and told Mrs. Bardell that Dodson and Fogg wished to see her at the office.

Mrs. Bardell, escorted by Tommy, Mrs. Sanders and Mrs. Cluppins, drove away.

An hour or so later, Mrs. Bardell alighted from the coach within the gates of the Fleet Prison.

From The Spaniards to Jack Straw's Castle is a pleasant walk along the crest of

The Spaniards. Garden

the hill with, on a clear day, fine views across Hampstead Heath, bounded by the great grey cloud of London, growing less and less distinct until it merges into the sky that comes down to meet it.

From Doughty Street across Hampstead Heath was a favourite walk with Dickens. He would send a hurried note to John Forster and walk him at a great pace across the

Heath to a place where " a red-hot chop and a bottle of good wine " could be obtained. This was Jack Straw's Castle, and Forster, who was short and rather stout, must, many a time, have been very glad to reach the immedate vicinity of the " red-hot chop."

From Jack Straw's Castle it is about a mile to Hampstead, where the Underground Railway will take you back to town.

It is an appropriate coincidence that the end of our journey should have taken us to a point where all London can be seen spread before us like a mammoth stage.  Dickens made it his own ; and produced his hundreds of characters, ordinary men and women,

Jack Straw's Castle
  Hampstead.

such as we rub shoulders with every day in the streets or in the trains, tramcars and omnibuses.  Outwardly they are in a greater hurry over their lawful, or unlawful occasions, but inwardly they are the same, some poor, some rich, some generous, some mean ; and those who have the eyes, can still find Mr. Podsnap and Mr. Pecksniff, Sam Weller and Montague Tigg.  And there are hundreds of Micawbers.  Neither is it impossible to find Betsey Trotwood and an occasional Peggotty, though, thanks to the man who brought them behind the footlights, the Gamps and Prigs, in so far as their former avocation goes, have retired into private life, along with Mr. and Mrs. Squeers. Who among us does not number a Mrs. Nickleby among our relatives or acquaintances ? She and the hundreds of others, who for nearly a century have been a lasting joy to the English-speaking peoples, are still in the streets or under the roofs dominated by that great dome rising above the murk.

He who drew their portraits with such uncanny insight and unerring skill, lies in the Abbey Church, whose twin towers you may see far to the west.

To give one last quotation from his friend, John Forster :

" He would himself have preferred to lie in the small graveyard under Rochester Castle wall, or in the little churches of Cobham or Shorne ; but all these were found to be closed ; and the desire of the Dean and Chapter of Rochester to lay him in their Cathedral had been entertained, when the Dean of Westminster's request, and the considerate kindness of his generous assurance that there should be only such ceremonial as would strictly obey all injunctions of privacy, made it a grateful duty to accept that offer. The spot already had been chosen by the Dean ; and before midday on the following morning, Tuesday the 14th of June, with the knowledge of those only who took part in the burial, all was done. . . ."

The stone placed on the grave is inscribed

## CHARLES DICKENS

BORN FEBRUARY THE SEVENTH, 1812, DIED JUNE THE NINTH, 1870.

# INDEX